What Do You Find in a Rainforest Tree?

Megan Kopp

Crabtree Publishing Company
www.crabtreebooks.com

Ecosystems
Close-Up

Author
Megan Kopp

Publishing plan research and development
Reagan Miller

Editors
Janine Deschenes
Crystal Sikkens

Design
Ken Wright
Tammy McGarr (cover)

Photo research
Janine Deschenes
Crystal Sikkens

Production coordinator and prepress technician
Ken Wright

Print coordinator
Katherine Berti

Photographs
iStockphoto.com: page 22
Minden Pictures/Superstock: page 17
Wikimedia Commons: Jake L. Snaddon, Edgar C. Turner and
    William A. Foster: page 21
All other images from Shutterstock

Library and Archives Canada Cataloguing in Publication

Kopp, Megan, author
    What do you find in a rainforest tree? / Megan Kopp.

(Ecosystems close-up)
Includes index.
Issued in print and electronic formats.
ISBN 978-0-7787-2261-8 (bound).--ISBN 978-0-7787-2281-6 (paperback).--
ISBN 978-1-4271-1725-0 (html)

    1. Rain forest animals--Juvenile literature. 2. Rain forest ecology--
Juvenile literature. I. Title.

QH541.5.R27K67 2016   j591.734   C2015-907992-6
                                               C2015-907993-4

Library of Congress Cataloging-in-Publication Data

Names: Kopp, Megan, author.
Title: What do you find in a rainforest tree? / Megan Kopp.
Description: Crabtree Publishing Company, [2016] | Series: Ecosystems
  close-up | Includes index.
Identifiers: LCCN 2015047297 | ISBN 9780778722618 (reinforced library
  binding) | ISBN 9780778722816 (pbk.) | ISBN 9781427117250 (electronic)
Subjects: LCSH: Rain forest animals--Juvenile literature. | Rain forest
  ecology--Juvenile literature.
Classification: LCC QL112 .K67 2016 | DDC 578.730913--dc23
LC record available at http://lccn.loc.gov/2015047297

Crabtree Publishing Company
www.crabtreebooks.com   1-800-387-7650

Printed in Canada/032016/EF20160210

Published in Canada
Crabtree Publishing
616 Welland Ave.
St. Catharines, Ontario
L2M 5V6

Published in the United States
Crabtree Publishing
PMB 59051
350 Fifth Avenue, 59th Floor
New York, New York 10118

Published in the United Kingdom
Crabtree Publishing
Maritime House
Basin Road North, Hove
BN41 1WR

Published in Australia
Crabtree Publishing
3 Charles Street
Coburg North
VIC 3058

Contents

What is a Rainforest?

Rainforests are warm, thick jungles that get a lot of rain. Tall trees and lots of plants grow in rainforests. Many different kinds of animals live in rainforest trees.

A rainforest tree is home to both this saimiri, or "squirrel" monkey, left, and the poison dart frog, above.

Rainforest Life

Rainforest trees are home to many living things. Plants and animals are living things. Living things change as they grow. They make new living things. Plants create new plants. Animals have babies. Rainforests also have nonliving things. They are not alive, and do not grow or change.

A Rainforest Tree Ecosystem

Systems are made up of many parts. These parts are connected and work together. If you take one part away, the system does not work very well.

In a rainforest tree ecosystem, all living and nonliving things are connected.

Sun

kapok tree

rain water

butterfly

quetza

butterfly

mccaw

dragonfly

toucan   butterfly

snake

hummingbird

snake

spider

tree frog   tree frog

plants

To understand how the living and nonliving things in a rainforest tree are connected, scientists might use **models**, such as this computer diagram.

A Rainforest Tree is a System

An **ecosystem** is a type of system. It includes all the living and nonliving things found in one place. They are all connected. A rainforest tree is a type of ecosystem.

Life in a Rainforest Tree

All living things have certain needs that must be met in order to **survive**, or stay alive. Living things can only survive in ecosystems that meet all of their needs.

Orchids are flowers that get everything they need to survive in a rainforest tree ecosystem.

What Do They Need?

Living things need both nonliving and other living things in order to stay alive. Plants need air, water, and sunlight to make their own food. This food gives them **energy** to grow. Animals need water, air, food, and **shelter** to survive.

Sloths depend on rainforest trees for food and shelter.

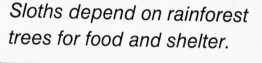

What do you Think?

Name three needs that all living things must have to survive.

Breathe Deep

All living things need air to live. Air is a nonliving thing. It is found all around a rainforest tree ecosystem. Plants need air, sunlight, and water to make food. Most plants in a rainforest use roots in the ground to take in water and **nutrients**. Some plants do not have roots. These plants, called air plants, live on rainforest trees.

Air plants use their leaves to take in water and nutrients from the air and rain.

Taking Air In

Animals take in air in different ways. Monkeys and birds, such as the brightly-colored toucan, take in air through their lungs. Rainforest frogs breathe in air through their skin.

Rainforest snakes, such as this green tree python, breathe using lungs.

What do you Think?

Look at the information on this page. How are living and nonliving things in a rainforest tree ecosystem connected?

Lots of Water

Living things need water to survive. A rainforest is a place where rain falls almost every day. Many plants soak up water through their roots.The kapok tree is a tall tree found in the Amazon Rainforest. It has a large trunk and roots.

Kapok trees can grow up to 13 feet (4 meters) in one year.

trunk

A Very Wet Rainforest!

Air plants grow on the branches, trunks, and leaves of trees. They get water from the **moist** air. Monkeys get water from the food they eat. Some animals, such as jaguars, drink water from puddles or streams.

Rainforest monkeys can get a lot of water from eating fruit.

What do you Think?

What do you think would happen to the rainforest tree ecosystem if it stopped raining?

Hungry, Anyone?

All living things need food to survive. Food gives them energy to grow. Plants use sunlight, air, and water to make their own food. Animals cannot make their own food. They must eat other living things to get the energy they need to survive.

Tall trees in a rainforest get a lot of sunlight and rain.

Dinnertime!

Three-toed sloths get their energy by eating the leaves and fruit of rainforest trees. Eagles hunt and eat other animals, such as sloths, to get the energy they need. A **food chain** shows how energy moves from one living thing to another in an ecosystem.

What do you Think?

How do eagles depend on rainforest trees?

This picture shows a rainforest tree food chain. The arrows show the flow of energy.

plants

sloth

eagle

Shelter in a Tree

Animals in a rainforest tree depend on both living and nonliving things for shelter. Animals need shelter for many reasons. It can protect animals from bad weather. It can also be a safe place to hide from other animals that may want to eat them.

Kookaburras use the leaves of a rainforest tree as shelter from the rain.

Many Uses

Animals might also use shelter as a place to lay eggs or raise babies. Eagles build nests high up in rainforest trees. This protects the chicks from animals that look for food close to the ground. The chicks stay near the nest for up to a year.

What do you Think?

Name two ways these harpy eagles depend on rainforest trees for shelter.

This harpy eagle mother has built a nest out of branches for her chick.

Losing our Rainforests

One tree supports many types of plants and animals. However, rainforests are disappearing fast. We are losing rainforests at the rate of about 4,000 football fields an hour.

Every single tree lost hurts all of the living things that depend on it.

Trees in Danger

The Amazon is the world's largest rainforest. Many trees are being cut down for wood and to clear land for buildings, towns, and farming. Large areas are being cut down faster than new areas can grow back.

What do you Think?

What do you think happened to the animals that lived in this part of the Amazon Rainforest when it got cut down?

Build a Rainforest Tree

A model is a **representation** of a real object. A model can show how different parts of an ecosystem work together. Models can also show how an ecosystem looks. Maps, pictures, storyboards, and diagrams are kinds of models.

Look at the next page to find out how to make your own model.

Create your Model

Draw a diagram of a rainforest ecosystem to show how living things meet their needs. Remember that living things need both living and nonliving things to survive. Make sure you add labels to your diagram.

This checklist shows what your diagram should include:
- 3 living things
- 3 nonliving things

air

Sun

tree

toucan

butterfly

iguana

leopard

spider

water

flower

Reach for Answers

Scientists use models to help them learn more about the systems they study. Now it is your turn! Share your model diagram with your classmates. Explain how each living thing on your diagram gets what it needs from the living and nonliving things in the rainforest tree ecosystem.

What do you Think?

Could the living things on your diagram survive in a different ecosystem? For example, could they meet their needs in a desert ecosystem? Why or why not?

Learning more

Books

Duke, Kate. *In the Rainforest (Let's-Read-and-Find-Out Science 2)*. Scholastic: New York, NY. 2014.

Goldner, Rita. *Orangutan: A Day in the Rainforest Canopy.* Dancing Dakini Press: Sedona, AZ. 2015.

Llewellyn, Claire & Thea Feldman. *Kingfisher Readers L2: In the Rainforest.* Macmillan Publishers: New York, NY. 2014.

Websites

Rainforest Alliance: Kid's Corner
www.rainforest-alliance.org/kids

National Geographic Kids: 15 Cool Things about Rainforests!
www.ngkids.co.uk/science-and-nature/15-cool-things-about-rainforests

Tropical Forest Biome
http://tropicalrainforestscience10.weebly.com/index.html

Enchanted Learning: Rainforest Activities
www.enchantedlearning.com/subjects/rainforest/Activities.shtml

Words to know

ecosystem (EE-koh-sis-tuhm) noun All the living things in a place and their relation to the environment

energy (EN-ur-jee) noun The ability to do things

food chain (food cheyn) noun The order of living things in an ecosystem by which food energy is passed from one to another

model (MOD-l) noun A representation of a real object

moist (moist) adjective Slightly wet

nutrients (noo-tree-uh nts) noun Natural substances that help plants and animals grow

representation (rep-ri-zen-TEY-shuh-n) noun A picture, drawing, model, or other copy of something

shelter (SHEL-ter) noun The place where living things are safe

survive (ser-VAHYV) verb To stay alive

A noun is a person, place, or thing. A verb is an action word that tells you what someone or something does. An adjective is a word that tells you what something is like.

Index